The Winning Personality:

A Values-Based Approach to Entrepreneurship In This Economy

James A. Hendrick Jr.

Copyright © 2015, 2019 James A. Hendrick Jr.

All rights reserved.

ISBN: 978 17969 13996

DEDICATION

This book is dedicated to my mother, Betty Jo Seibold, who helps bring out the best in me everyday, and to my late best friend Keith Cotton, 1963-2003.

CONTENTS

	Introduction	Pg 1
1	Chapter 1 - What is this Winning Personality?	Pg 4
2	Chapter 2 - Maybe It's Leadership	Pg 11
3	Chapter 3 - Creativity is Crucial	Pg 17
4	Chapter 4 - Determination and Discipline	Pg 24
5	Chapter 5 - Personality and Character	Pg 32
6	Chapter 6 - Faith	Pg 38
7	Chapter 7 - Setting Goals	Pg 45
8	Chapter 8 - Business Needs Networking	Pg 52
9	Chapter 9 - A Winning Personality Serves	Pg 58
10	Chapter 10 - Adversity to Go!	Pg 64
	Epilogue	Pg 72

ACKNOWLEDGMENTS

These people have shaped my thinking and helped me over the years begin to find the point where I begin to chase my destiny:

Robert Kiyosaki
Dr. John C. Maxwell
Dr. Stephen Covey
Anthony Robbins
Donald Trump
John F. Kennedy
Ronald Reagan
Rush Limbaugh
President Thomas S. Monson
Elder Jeffrey R. Holland
Elder Boyd K. Packer
Elder D. Todd Christofferson
President Russell M. Nelson

These pastors have shaped my spiritual development over the year:

Pastor Jim Sellers of Midessa Heights Baptist Church
Pastor Frank Laceter of University Heights Baptist Church
Pastor John Strapazon of First Baptist Lubbock
Pastor Walter Sanders of Rehoboth Baptist Church
Pastor Weeks DuBose at Westwood Baptist Church
Bishop Chris Vore
Bishop James Johnson
Bishop Steven Crooks
Bishop Thomas Kimball
Bishop Michael Winfrey
Bishop Brian Gwilliam
Bishop David and Sister Emily Martin

INTRODUCTION

I came up with this book idea after numerous blog posts that I have made over the past month and a half. I will be drawing from some of those blog posts as well as other insights. As an aspiring entrepreneur and speaker, I have found that those who are successful hold to this personality type.

A winning entrepreneur should chase more than money. Delatorro McNeal and Robert Kiyosaki say, "Too many people chase the almighty dollar instead of their Almighty Destiny, that gift that God has inside that's just bursting at the seams to come out." Sure, we all need money to provide for our needs, but the true entrepreneur gets out of the survival mentality- it's not a good environment for them. They must also get out of the entitlement mentality. My father always would say, "James, there ain't no free lunch in this world." He was a member of the baby boomer generation who worked hard. He worked for nearly 40 years in the oilfields trying to make a decent living for our family, almost as long as I've been alive. Entitlement was not part of his vocabulary.

I also believe that a good entrepreneur must put his or her best foot forward. My mother and maternal grandfather always told me, "James, always try your best, and people will know." Quality was a value distilled in me from my mother's side of the family. Granddad always said, "IF something's worth doing, it's worth doing right." My Granddad owned his own business, a brake and alignment repair shop, for five years. He passed on to me the entrepreneurial spirit.

As you read this book, I hope you can use the inspirational advice to help you chart a course-a course to chase your Almighty Destiny! Jim Rohn declared, " If you don't design your own life plan, chances are you'll fall into someone else's plan. And guess what they have planned for you? Not much."

At this writing, it's Sunday evening, and I had learned earlier today that people of faith must chart a course in their lives, and this course must include the Lord. If you are not a true person of faith, this book is not for you.

People with the winning personality are not free from adversity. I've learned through hard experience when I was seriously knocked down by a divorce that it's your choices that get you through adversity. It's applying your faith, putting it into action. As James says "Even so, faith, if it hath not works is dead, being alone." (James 5:17, King James Version)

So if you have the faith to rise above adversity, then you have the winning personality, and this book is most definitely for you. Otherwise, you wouldn't have bothered to buy it or pick it up. If you have the foresight to forge a path with the entrepreneurial spirit, then all systems are go, and you can proceed forward with this book.

This book can give you insight. I wish to take each of you on a daring adventure that God can help you forge. You can be pioneers in your family, in your faith community, and in your community at large. America needs people who are entrepreneurs, striving for greatness, and I am one of them.

Let me qualify something. I am a man of simple means, I'm just starting this journey, and I plan to start this journey with you. The insights in this book will be things I have learned and will continue to learn as it is written.

I am a simple man. I studied Speech and Mass Communications at the University of Texas of the Permian Basin, I also minor in Business Management. I wish to translate my two loves, entrepreneurship and public speaking into a great chase for my destiny.

I believe God has a special destiny for you. And I also believe that God designed happiness in the plan for each and every one of us. My faith has a unique view of why God put us on this planet, and I hope to share some insights from that as well.

You need to create a project that carves your destiny. Dr. John C Maxwell says "Following your passion changes your life and the lives of those around you. It makes life exciting. It inspires your team. It transforms the grind of work into an invigorating challenge."
In my mid-forties I've just discovered my passion-writing and speaking to audiences in the hopes of empowering them in their challenges. As an old adage says: "Adversity builds character."

I've seen adversity build character in my life. When I was 24, I had life planned out. I was going to go to Texas Tech University, graduate with a degree in Broadcast Journalism and become a radio talk show host, marry my sweetheart, and move to Dallas to be near my late best friend while building a career and a family. Well, after a few hard knocks from clowning around, I switched my major to Political Science. I was going to be a lawyer and politician. I was on the fast track to law school. Then I got sick.

As mentioned above, my marriage deteriorated, but if it hadn't my faith wouldn't have developed the way it is today. After my friend died, I tried a brief stint in graduate school, but it wasn't for me. So I opted for a second Bachelor's in Communication-at least until I become a speaker.

Dr. Maxwell also says following your passion helps you in the daily grind of work. I can't count some mornings when I woke up not really wanting to go to school. I will share you my secret to overcoming the "I don't feel like it" condition later in this book. I've seen days where I complained, "This morning is tedious-I just don't feel like going!" The secret is simple if you work it. So I wish to chase my destiny instead. Being a student is cool, but I'd rather write books and speeches rather than term papers.

You can't put a price on self-actualization, and I've seen it pay off, because I pay the price through sweat and tears as I push for my dream. I say this following statement not out of sarcasm (I'm not one for sarcasm), but out of passion. Ain't the American Dream Grand! So let's do this!

CHAPTER 1 -
WHAT IS THIS WINNING PERSONALITY?
BASIC CHARACTERISTICS OF AN AMBIVERT

What is this "Winning Personality?" Well I've been searching for the answers for quite awhile. I've taken the Myers-Briggs test three times and came out an extrovert. But the reality is that the winning personality is somewhere in between the Introvert/Extrovert spectrum.

According to a featured article in the March 2015 Entrepreneur Magazine, the writer stated that no leader is in either extreme of the Introvert/Extrovert spectrum. Even Donald Trump, who is obviously an extrovert, has his own idiosyncrasies of introversion. I've seen this in the lives of some of my favorite heroes struggled with them as well. Abraham Lincoln was one of the greatest President of the United States, dealt with serious depression where he seemed withdrawn. John F. Kennedy, once gregarious, was changed by World War 2. I mean he loved speaking to audiences and ran for public office, but in his compartmentalized personality was somewhat of an introvert. He never wanted to talk about his heroism during the war.

I've faced this reality in life. At one time, I was an extreme extrovert. But over time, facing some rejection and trauma, I became a little more shy. I tried three network marketing business models, but I couldn't get the gumption to make sales calls.

The winning personality is the Ambivert. You can still succeed in business with this personality, if you just get out there to make things happen in your business. According to the data I researched, winning entrepreneurs have this personality, and can with a little elbow grease make things happen for their own businesses!

I'm preaching to myself and anybody who is fortunate to read this book. Over my 45 years in life, I have seen wealthy entrepreneurs I've had the pleasure to meet learn to overcome their insecurities. I've struggled with that myself. In the 1990's, I was involved with an awesome business model. In doing presentations, my ex-wife, whom I was dating at the time, found my presentations to be "too nervous." I felt like I could have helped her monetize, but her extreme extroverted personality and absolute fear got in the way, and as a result, I became a little more introverted.

Let me qualify this with the featured article. One thing the writer was trying to say that not all extroverts make good leaders, and I believe they had the statistics to back it up. But we don't need statistics, just look around.

Back when I was in that business model, I was too extroverted. A coach in the model always said, "Until you've done enough in this model to coach, try to say few words." And that is my motto. That's why at my last Students in Free Enterprise (hereafter SIFE) (now named Enactus) meeting, I didn't say much. I let the students who had the experience do the talking, then stepped up to the plate to be their Project Manager the next year. If you're a student with aspirations to be an entrepreneur, I highly recommend Enactus.

Defining Terms

OK, at this point you're probably saying "Jimmy, are you nuts? Why do you need to define terms?" Well I like to do this in any writing I'm passionate about so that I can take the terms defined and further elaborate. I said this was a great adventure, right? But I digress. In their 4th edition of Fundamentals of Contemporary Management, authors Jones and George define an extrovert as a person with a "tendency to positive feelings about himself and the world around them" (Jones & George p 47). No doubt I'm an extrovert, but not as much as when I was younger. Hard times knocked the extreme extroversion out of me, and maybe I'm a bit more balanced, if I can just overcome the fear, which I will. More on overcoming fear in a later chapter. I also define an extrovert as social and sanguine. To me, an introvert is someone with the tendency to isolate, to keep to themselves, perhaps out of a lack of trust. I have a bit of that personality, though not as much.

Now, I must define the term ambivert. An ambivert is someone in the middle with enough extroversion to get his name out, but enough introversion to keep quiet about some things until they actually make it. As the March 2015 edition of Entrepreneur magazine said, ambiverts fall somewhere in the middle of the spectrum. And folks, that's how I define myself. So, if you're going to be a good entrepreneur, you're going to need to become an ambivert. Period. End of story.

My Ambivert Philosophy

OK, maybe I need to back it up and explain. The rest of this book is going to tell you how to be an effective ambivert through mastering various concepts, so take notes. Be sure to self-actualize and take good notes, because like I said, this is a journey. There's more to an entrepreneur than just opening a business to make money- you've got to define yourself, define your brand, your attitudes, values, and culture you wish your organization to have.

You need to decide today what are your talents as an ambivert and entrepreneur to hone them. That is the only way you can chase your destiny. You need to decide and realize today that adversity often comes, and you have to find a way to sharpen your brand and fine tune your product, which is what I am currently doing at this writing.

Let me give you an ultimate vision of my company. I wish to sell health products as well as books to empower, inspire, and motivate people.

I'm sure like me you have God-given talents. Like an ambivert, it's your job to discover them and take your journey no matter what bumps of adversity hits your way.

The fact is people can use their talents to help themselves become rich. I'd like to help the poor, give them a hand up without looking down on them, because they may have talents they could hone and monetize.

At this writing, it is now the wee hours of the morning. So since this may bring forth my best writing now, I'll give you some insights. To me, the words 'ambivert' and 'arrogance' just don't go together. I pray often that God will bless my future business enterprises, but I ask that if He allows it, that He would help me stay humble. I want to help the poor get hand ups to get good paying jobs. More advice like this may appear later in this book. God blesses us with so many things, attributes, and virtues. So if you've defined yourself as an ambivert, this book is definitely for you! If not, there's still hope. I'll be covering the ambivert in many aspects of the book.

Ambiverts must have the gumption to get the word out in their business, especially in this economy. But I think an ambivert must be quiet enough not to make a fool of himself. I had no problem being extroverted, but hard knocks made me somewhat reserved over the years. So I guess I fit right in. Maybe you can too.

Ambiverts must be willing to sacrifice, give up mindless TV, watching only informative and inspirational shows. In my adult life, I've only watched shows where I could learn, both temporal and spiritual lessons. Another thing they might sacrifice is sleep. In fact, at this writing, I've only had 2 hours of sleep, because I was getting my creative juices going.

Sometimes I give up lunches when I go to school, so I can attend class and work on assignments. Lunch will come after the work is done.

Ten years ago, I was involved in another business model. I went to my mentor's house to receive some coaching. We watched Star Trek for a little while. Then he had a question. "Do you realize that luxury cars like the BMW, the Jaguar, or Mercedes aren't advertised on TV?" he asked.

"As a matter of fact, I have noticed."

"That's because the rich don't watch much TV at all. So if you watch TV, make sure you learn something from it."

Unfortunately, timidity and shyness, along with tough peer pressure caused me to lack interest in this particular business model. An ambivert must learn that when he fails, the true winning personality gets back up, and that's what I did.

The ambivert must also be armed with personal development tools. In his book, The 21 Irrefutable Laws of Leadership , Dr. Maxwell's mentor suggested a personal development program through reading books and listening to CDs and watching DVDs. These kinds of programs should cause the ambivert to dig deep into his personality and come again with his business sales team to make it happen. I mean really and seriously, if you want to get successful, then start reading books, get into books and read those that help you grow. Put your business into high gear, ditch the TV watching for a bit, and pay attention to positive people around you. The ones that you love may not understand at the beginning. But I guarantee they will. After all, people will see the changes and will want to follow you.

Ambiverts must also be persistent and persevere. Dr. John Maxwell speaks to large audiences as well as one on one mentoring. He says, "I try to instill in [people] a belief in themselves until my belief becomes their own belief in themselves." A leader and a motivator must foster a strong belief in themselves, because otherwise audiences cannot be persuaded.

I recall an incident in my life. It was between my sophomore and junior year. I was rustling about trying to get accepted into Texas Tech University, getting things squared away in housing. For awhile, it did not look good. But then I buckled down and got faith in God. He put the belief in myself. Friends said "Jimmy, you're making a big mistake. You won't make it in Lubbock." Yet I persisted. I got the acceptance letter, and for a while housing was pacified.

That is not to say I didn't have hard times later. But this one experience back in the summer of 1994 helped me muster faith in myself and in God until I got my first Bachelor's degree, a feat that some experts said was impossible for me.

I have another experience that called for persistence and perseverance. In the 1988-89 school year, I was a sophomore on Permian High School's swimming team. I was a junior varsity swimmer performing the 50 yard freestyle. The invitational meet was in Abilene, which was about three hours away from where I live. I woke up at 4 that morning and headed for the bus at the school (my parents drove me there). By the time of my competition in the qualifying heat, it was late morning/early afternoon. I was in Heat 1 Lane 4 (for those of you who know about the sport of swimming). I was very nervous until the adrenaline kicked in. I was tired at the 25th yard, but my teammates and the coach (We'll call him Coach W.) cheered me on. I made it all the way to the end of the lap. Although I won no trophies, Coach W. told me on the bus that there was a standing ovation for me. A true leader must endure.

Ambivert leaders must make a covenant with themselves, their organizations and their God to pursue excellence. In his paper, Leonard Moisan declared that, "We have a leadership crisis in our country" (Moisan L Leadership is a covenant, Journal of Business Disciplines Vol 2 No 1). I will discuss my view on an ambivert's faith and leadership.

An an ambivert, you must have some great people skills. I've been to conventions and seminars where entrepreneurs said, "If you want to succeed in business, you have to love the people you serve in your organization." I will go through more on people skills in the leadership and other chapters of this book. But let's face it. If you don't have people skills, chances are you get nothing out of your business. Your mentors won't waste time helping you develop the people skills you refuse to have. Your fellow entrepreneurs will leave you in the dust. Face it, ambiverts live on people skills.

If God has given you the entrepreneurial spirit, and if you're a true ambivert with a vision and a passion. you will have a winning personality.

CHAPTER 2 -
MAYBE IT'S LEADERSHIP

What is leadership? I've been grappling with a definition of the term leadership for almost 20 years. That is why I was intrigued when I stumbled across a feature article in the March 2015 issue of Entrepreneur Magazine. Raymond Hennesey, editor of the online edition of Entrepreneur states that the real leaders are those who take action. But John Maxwell, best selling author of Thinking for a Change qualifies that "Real leaders take action, but their action is based on their thinking."

A technical definition of leadership is found in the 4th edition of the textbook Essentials in Contemporary Management. The authors define leadership as, "The process by which an individual influences other people." Dr. John Maxwell simplifies that definition in his book The 21 Irrefutable Laws of Leadership by saying that, "The essence of leadership is influence, nothing more, nothing less." In that book, Dr. Maxwell suggests prospective leaders should volunteer in an organization for a year to test their leadership skills.

I must interject my faith here. As a member of The Church of Jesus Christ of Latter-day Saints, we have an unpaid ministry. In the 13 1/2 years I've been a member, I've been a Sunday School teacher, a Quorum Secretary in the Priesthood, a Priest Advisor to Young Men, among other things. What I've got to say is this, you may have billions of dollars and have shares in holding companies and consulting firms, but if you have a pompous way of thinking, you're not a true leader. I agree with Dr. Maxwell, a leader must have a servant's heart! A leader must have faith to persevere in what he believes is the best influence for his organization. Yes, leaders take action, but it's all in their thinking, faith, and attitude that they influence others.

When I think of a business leader who led and inspired through adversity, it is Heber J. Grant, the seventh president of the Church of Jesus Christ of Latter-Day Saints. His father died shortly after he was born, and at a young age, he began working as a business clerk to care for his mother. He was excited about a career in the Navy, but agreed to sacrifice that to go into business to take care of his mother, and later his family. Adversity struck Grant hard in his life. The Panic of 1893 wiped out his savings and business income. Not only that, but he was in debt. Nonetheless, he used the courage in business leadership to wade through that time and in a few years, his business revived.

Now let's look at another issue, leadership vs management. I wish to help define leadership and juxtapose it with the definition and theory of management. Management is the ability to guide, lead, and control human resources. Leadership is the ability to persuade, influence, and inspire others to follow a certain plan.

I think about some of the leaders in my life. I have a friend (Let's call him Ron). I won't go into too much of what he does, but I see him as a great leader in church, in the home, and in business. He is one of the most humble men I've ever met.

Leadership has always been a powerful topic for me ever since I was 12. Sensing this, my maternal grandmother saw potential in me "to be my little preacher." Well in a way, as an ecclesiastical priesthood holder, I am. But as I said before, it's a lay, voluntary, unpaid ministry, a foreign concept to some people. It keeps us humble.

Management, although studied in colleges and universities, can be an outdated model. Today, there are more books on leadership than management. That's why Odessa College in Odessa, Texas changed its Management Program to the Leadership Program. Wise choice!

In some cases, management and leadership go hand in hand. The President/CEO of a company is often a leader, depending on whether he or she is the founder of the company. Robert Kiyosaki in his book Rich Dad's Cashflow Quadrant states that while "Management is only a tool skill for business," but leadership "brings out the best in people."

Pick a Side: Leadership or Management

Now I will tell you the truth of how I feel. As an aspiring entrepreneur, I don't have a staff. But if I do end up with one, I want to lead, not manage! There may be some entrepreneurs who have made it, and made millions. But they look down at everyone - their staff, and people in general. That is old-style poor management!

I've sat at conferences where a wealthy entrepreneur has told audiences, "If you become wealthy and forget where you came from, God will make sure you go right back there." I will always see to it that I remember where I came from.

Dr. Stephen Covey says, "The best leaders are not at the top of the org charts looking down at their staff. The best leaders are on the ground, helping their people get to the next level." I firmly believe in this.

Suppose you asked me which form of leading I would pick for an entrepreneur with a winning personality. I would have to choose leadership over management. Dr. John Maxwell clearly said, "Managers want things to stay the same, but leaders want things to change." If I were to launch an empowerment consulting business, I would want to lead my employees, and make them partners. This to me would signify equality. My motto would be, "If we all push together, we will achieve our team's goal." That's what a leader would do.

A good leader has to have good people skills. I have not met a wealthy entrepreneur who does not have people skills to guide his or her organization. In my last relationship, my ex-wife displayed poor people skills and embarrassed the business organization we were part of. Those people in my past organization turned to me and said, "Why can't she be like you? You are so good with people and an inspiration to us."

In management, the term 'human resources' comes to mind when you think of people skills. 'Human resources' is an arcane word used to keep corporate employees a cog in the work system. I prefer "partnership" and "adding value to people" as more modern terms an entrepreneur needs to succeed in people skills.

Leaders need to be good with words. In Rich Dad's Cashflow Quadrant, Kiyosaki's Rich Dad said, "If you want to be a leader of many, you have to be a master of words." If you looked at leadership guru and Harvard Business School Professor John Kotter, a leader's urgency doesn't come from a PowerPoint presentation, it comes from the heart. This is from his book, A Sense of Urgency.

I have studied Political Science and Public Relations, and I have found a few great communicators. Theodore Roosevelt, FDR, John F. Kennedy, and Ronald Reagan communicated hope. Business communicators like Steve Jobs, the late Dr. Stephen Covey, and Mark Zuckerberg have communicated their brand and brand ideals.

Entrepreneurial communication is a pioneer field according to Business Communication scholar Dale Cyphert. He said the speech of certain professionals is "different from the speech of an entrepreneur." Yet in my research I have observed that scholars don't study the field, they just observe those who are using their ways with words. Masters of words are key in the marketplace.

An entrepreneur who wants to lead must also master interpersonal or one on one communication in collaboration and coaching. A leader must become an effective coach on one on one situations.

I think that Business Administration/Management is an interchangeable and obsolete term. For entrepreneurs who want training in college, emphasis is needed on Business. A CEO ambivert must master top leadership skills and leave the Industrial Age-obsolete model behind until the field reforms itself into an Information/Creation Age mode.

An entrepreneur who desires to be a leader must be patient. I can't count the number of business audios calling fellow entrepreneurs in the audience to be patient. Entrepreneurship is a process for the business and the organization therein to grow. You have the potential to become a great leader someday as an entrepreneur. It begins like a seed, so don't sabotage the growth of your business and organization.

In my volunteer job I had almost fifteen years ago, I encountered a manager who seemed to have little patience with her employees. Her personality had a lot of grit, and I would categorize her as an "active negative" leader. Don't get me wrong, active negative leaders do get things done. The problem is, I see very little patience in this personality. Some examples of active negative leaders in politics are Lyndon Johnson and Richard Nixon.

Entrepreneurs need to exercise a particle of patience in order to allow their organizations and businesses to grow. I have met a few entrepreneurs who had the patience in dealing with people, and their organizations grew. I have met many entrepreneurs who were good with people, great communicators, but they lacked patience with their people to help them grow and develop. I can't say it more emphatically, an entrepreneur who says he has a sound leadership philosophy, but he treats people in his organization and family with impatience, is not a leader.

CHAPTER 3-

FOR AMBIVERTS, CREATIVITY IS CRUCIAL

As an aspiring author and speaker, creativity is my bread and butter. Any entrepreneurial venture requires some creativity, namely in the fields of Advertising, Marketing, and Public Relations. This is where finding and shaping your brand is compelling. The rubber meets the road here!

At first in a business, the entrepreneur is solely responsible for bringing out his/her product or service so the business can survive. Later as it grows, you need a manager who is also creative.

There was a study by a sociologist at Princeton University who examined students graduating from business school at Stanford University. The majority wanted to be entrepreneurs and start their own businesses. What he found out was that the most successful entrepreneurs meet with those of different professions to gain insight regarding what they need to innovate new products and services.

You know in large corporations, they have skunkworks (little organizations inside of the corporate organization). But if you're the only one calling the shots in your business, it's up to you to become creative on your business message and product/service trends. A good mastermind group could help you.

I recommended a regular brainstorming session with the people around you. They will give clarity for your creative vision. I love to brainstorm. It's ok doing it alone, but I love brainstorming as a team.

When I think of creative entrepreneurs, I think of Mark Zuckerberg (founder of Facebook) and the late Dr. Stephen Covey, motivational speaker and partner with Franklin Covey. When I listen in on conversations with future entrepreneurs, I want to know, "Who is your target audience?" The communicator in me wants to know these things in order to give them creative ideas to advertise and market their product or service.

Creative entrepreneurs must do a little market research. You need to know what your competitor is doing so that you can do it better. Entrepreneurs should take this research and segment down to your target audience, and determine how to reach them. I recommend research marketing as a tool to gain more profits for your company. Listening to competitors and employees go a long way. In fact, communication scholars believe that poor listening skills crashes businesses and interpersonal relationships. If you want to grow in your passion, you need to be a great listener.

Recently, I watched a Ted Talk by Glenn Gaudette. He showed the creative/innovative entrepreneur model, and it was clear that creativity is the base. You cannot be an innovative entrepreneur without being creative on how to promote your product and services in a way that no one has done before.

If you have a dream or passion, then you need to come up with creative ways to build your business. After all, as a speaker and entrepreneur, I try to come up with something new I can do every day. I took a Small Business Management class at the University of Texas Permian Basin. From studying my notes, I used to believe that entrepreneurs needed to become generalists to succeed in business. However, I now see that being a generalist can lead to failure.

I strongly oppose a cookie cutter one size fits all brand of creation. Your creativity must be original to keep clientele loyal. Let's use a hypothetical situation. Let's say I give a speech to a university or my church. With these, I would first consult the client, and ask what is the target demographic audience? In my business enterprise, my team needs synergy, which is the ability to coordinate together in a creative way. Even though I am the leader of my business, I would inform my team that it's time to have some creativity for the speech or project I want done for our client.

Let me give you part of my personal story. I was born legally blind. I grew up in the 1970's where few blind people were mainstreamed. Throughout my elementary school career, I was labeled "mentally challenged" and a "slow learner." It took a sixth grade teacher to show me that I was not what I had been labeled all those years. She spurred on my creativity. Now, I use my imagination to help others and make sense of the world. So if you want to be an effective entrepreneur, you need a good imagination. Otherwise, you ought to hire a staff member or bring in a new partner to bring imagination and creativity to your business.

Remember at the beginning of this book, I told you about the Myers-Briggs test. I took it almost nine years ago. You say, "How does that affect my creativity, Jimmy?" I'll tell you that the most creative entrepreneurs have an intuitive hunch. When I think of intuitive leaders, I think of Theodore Roosevelt, John F. Kennedy, and Ronald Reagan. When I think of creative entrepreneurs that are intuitive, I think of Bill Gates, Mark Zuckerberg, and Ted Turner. You don't have to have an intuitive personality to be creative, but it really helps.

The result of this and other testing showed that I was very creative and very passionate about what I'm doing. I think entrepreneurs need to be creative about marketing their passions to others who can help grow your brand and your business. I use my creative intuitive side of me to generate dialogue in any business or public setting.

As an ambivert, you need to seek out a life coach, a mentor who can be creative with you and consult with you on your strengths and weakness. These people, whether they be mentors, fellow entrepreneurs, or friends, will form a mastermind group to spur on your passion, with the hope that profits and quality increase.

I may have said it before in this chapter, but I'll say it again. I love brainstorming. I can do it by myself. but I prefer two or more to make brainstorming work. It is a powerful tool to help brand your product in a unique way.

Collaboration is great. The only risk with that, according to the December 2015 Entrepreneur Magazine is "somebody going rogue." With that, I highly recommend that you buy into a system of entrepreneurs who can help your creativity and hold you accountable at the same time. Network marketing and relationship marketing are powerful tool systems for your success.

As an entrepreneur who doesn't have much of an organization, you can't hire a team of skunkworks to toss around ideas in their heads. This is where I think you should buy into a system that would help you be more creative. In this case, much of the research and development is done for you. Two systems could be network marketing and franchising. In a system, you meet good quality people that are going to teach you the ins and outs of business by example. As the saying was coined while I attended university in the 1990's, "Been there, done that. Got the T-shirt." You need a mentor and a system and a mastermind to guide your creativity in business.

Recently, I spoke with a close friend of mine from church. She told me she and her family had gone to a local hockey game when she found a booth giving away cupcakes for free. Her curiosity led her to ask the reason behind this creativity. She told me it was a non-profit organization that made birthday cakes and threw birthday parties for impoverished children. When I think of that, I think of finding the nearest health fair for people to sample some of the product I may soon sell again and hear the story. Hopefully, you've grasped the concept that a brand must tell a creative story.

"The art of communication is the language of Leadership." -James Humes

One thing I neglected to mention is that creativity and leadership go hand in hand. You may ask, "Jimmy how do these two subjects relate?" Well, being a scholar in the field of communication, I learned that companies have their own organizational culture that helps package ideas. Good leaders need to be creative communicators.

Sometimes being creative involves communicating to your partners and staff a need to branch out into other markets. If you're a successful entrepreneur in one area you may be successful in another. Let's say a woman decides to do some public speaking, and then she decides to branch out into public relations. I believe that true entrepreneurs who want to be successful need to be creative in deciding whether to stick to one marketing plan or branch out.

Creativity: Difficult Work

I love creativity, but sometimes it often requires difficult work. You can't just say, "I have a wonderful idea," and go on with business as usual. It requires employees and partners to get involved in synergy to get the work done. The difficult work may require working late to improve on the idea. It may require Saturday to be a working day, for example. The economy doesn't care about your idea until you do the difficult work to make your created idea presentable.

Leaders of industries don't just come up with an idea and submit it to the marketplace unrevised. These leaders need to see if their idea matches with current trends in their respective industries. For example, a media consulting firm may have to test their ideas in different social media platforms. I currently have my business on Facebook and LinkedIn to network with others in my industry.

Let's say you need more sales leads for your media consulting firm.

Now, let's throw in a deadline to have a meeting regarding those leads. That means you will have to do difficult work to package your idea in the marketplace before any clients are willing to support your brand.

So if you need successful results on your creative idea, difficult work is needed to test and retool the product or service that is part of your new idea.

If you want to be a successful entrepreneur and in your personal life, you have to work hard. I didn't say this journey and this adventure is easy. But nothing that's easy is worthwhile. You have to do the work and count the cost, even if you're pouring everything you have into your idea.

At this point in reading, you are probably asking me, "Jimmy, what are you trying to say?" I am saying that if you want to succeed in your creative idea, you have to pay the price. There is always a price to pay for everything.

For you Americans, read these words. Freedom isn't free, a price had to be paid. The same way goes for the business world too. It requires discipline. More on discipline will be discussed in the next chapter.

Sometimes, doing the difficult work has to be done on your own. This will help you celebrate the small victories as well as the huge ones, because you did it.

In conclusion, your creative idea is your baby, especially if your business is a sole proprietorship. Your brand is you in that case. In corporations, the entrepreneur still has to have a full say on how the creative idea works. Why do you think have I spent so many hours to get this book to the point where it is today? Because I consulted a few people and did a little research. For authors, their book, their work product is their baby. You see, nothing that's easy and takes very little time is worthwhile. If you have a creative idea for the marketplace in your respective industry, you have to work hard.

But you ask, "How can hard work spur creativity?" There's the magical ingredient reported in Entrepreneurial Leadership. As I may have told you, I am author, podcaster, and motivational speaker. But I also think it would be nice to branch out into the field of Public Relations. That is going to take some time to work through. I have to focus on this one thing at a time.

CHAPTER 4 -

DETERMINATION AND DISCIPLINE: THE CRUX OF THE MATTER

"In life, you suffer two pains, the pain of discipline or the pain of regret." Jim Rohn.

"Can't could never do anything." Billie Jo Sawyer, my grandfather.

That last quote was from my maternal grandfather. I remember in childhood, the hours I spent talking to my grandfather while the other kids in the family went out to play. He'd talk about politics, history, the Bible, and business. Despite his faults, I think Granddad was a wise man. In childhood, he would always tell me, "James, you can do anything you set your mind to." This was in stark contradiction to what the "experts" tried to say. He knew I was no slow learner. He fought for me to have a normal education. Sadly, he didn't make it to my high school graduation. He had passed away a year and a half before that.

You guessed it, the first half of this chapter is on determination, then I will end it on the subject of discipline.

I can think of three times in my lifetime that I was determined to have something in my life.

Back in 1991, I was in a vocational rehab center for the blind in Austin. My caseworker and various "experts" wanted me to delay college and be there for six months. I bucked the system with everything I had, even though it tried to kick me back. It almost divided me from my family. Finally one afternoon, I was having lunch with friends who belonged to the National Federation of the Blind. One guy told me, "James, they have to give you the rehab package you want, it's the law." Another friend said, "If you have any more problems, let us know. We'll get the state affiliate of the Federation (hereafter NFB) involved."

Needless to say, the counselor at the center gave in, and I was college bound. I can't say it was easy; it was hard. I poured in seven years of blood, sweat, and tears and changing my major three times to get my first bachelor's degree.

There is another incident that occurred in 1994. I was back in the rehab center for more training. I was trying to get housing and other things set up to go to Texas Tech University in Lubbock, Texas. Friends and experts tried to get me to cave in. "Jimmy, just give up and go to college back home," a counselor said. Another friend said, "What makes you think you'll survive in Lubbock? You'll be on the streets in six months." Well, I used all my faith in God to bring to me some determination. I got accepted to Texas Tech University, and housing was satisfied for a time.

But there was one more time when determination was needed. I wanted to get an apartment in the same complex as my girlfriend (later my ex wife). I was told it would take time, because the apartments were booked. Well I prayed and fasted for three days, with my mother begging me to eat. I wouldn't eat until God satisfied my need. We drove to Lubbock not knowing what would happen. My parents thought I was crazy. But once again, it worked. My parents co-signed for the apartment which was across the way from my girl at the time. I felt like God had given me the victory.

Now some of you I know are probably saying, "Jimmy, how could you involve God in this? This is a book on business." My thought is this, if you need determination so your business can reach a goal, you must have faith in something to bring out the determination to work it out.

I will now give a hypothetical case study of an entrepreneur who was determined, based on a video I watched on YouTube. We'll call her Rene. She had the entrepreneurial spirit back in the third grade selling paper airplanes (great idea, I waited until I was 26 before deciding I want to be an entrepreneur). Rene studied marketing in college, but she could get no job afterwards, so she created her own job, a zero budget public relations operation. Her self-determination made her very successful in her business, and she is learning more about the industry as often as possible. Now that's what I call self-determination.

I am preaching to myself and anybody who wants to start a business, but when times are tough, often people fold. They cave in to the herd around them, the friends who say, "This will never work." I have found myself dealing with that as well. A lot of it on my part is dealing with fear. But that's when you need to move and overcome your fears. After all, financial expert Robert Kiyosaki called fear, "False Evidence Appearing Real."

Determination requires you to not quit and to keep an eye on a set goal. No matter how many times you've been knocked down, it's time to get up and work toward your goal. How do I know? I have been knocked down myself. I've had people who were once determined for me to succeed, then knock me down. Because of this, I think about what Delatorro McNeal told an audience, "If they're not there to share your story, they don't deserve to share your glory." Determination is needed to make it through hard times.

You've heard the old adage, "A winner never quits, and a quitter never wins." If you want to succeed as an entrepreneur among the big boys, determination is a must-have. No excuses, and no exception.

Let's say for an example, you own a small public relations firm, and your mentor is a life coach. Now let's say your life coach gives you a goal of 4 sales leads of clients to be done in 3 to four weeks. Now, the real test as to whether this firm is going to grow is the determination and nerve you have to get your business off the ground running.

You say, "Jimmy, why are you putting determination and discipline as one trait?" Well the truth is they are interrelated. You can't have one without the other. You may be determined to reach your goals, but do you have discipline? You may be disciplined in succeeding your at goals, but if you cave in to fear, you will lose determination.

Dr. John Maxwell says it best, "Self discipline is the thing that separates the successful and the non-successful." He used an analogy of two groups of people. The first group of people who say, "Let's wait until I feel like it." Chances are, that never happens. The second group says, "Let's go ahead and do this anyway so we will feel like it." To me, the latter gains momentum to succeed in business and any other endeavor in his or her life.

Self Discipline

This is a foundational habit for any entrepreneur. In fact, research shows that self discipline is a bedrock habit for success. I will be honest with you, that I am working on this area of my life. Some mornings, I wake up and don't feel like doing the things I need and want to do that day. But many times I think about what Delatorro McNeal says in his book Caught Between a Dream and a Job. "The world is ran by people who don't feel like it." But they do it anyway.

I mentioned this in my introduction, and I wish to elaborate. I bet President George W. Bush woke up in the White House sometimes not feeling like executing his duties. I bet Dr. Phil did not always feel like coming on his show. I'm sure that Donald Trump as an entrepreneur and real estate developer did not always feel like conducting business. But the reality is, these folks had discipline to help guide their success. You have to push yourself out the door and into your destiny.

Remember I quoted Jim Rohn earlier in my book. Rohn has another quote on discipline. "Discipline weighs ounces, while regret weighs tons." I've seen the tonnage regret has had on my life over the years. But, I have also seen the sweet ounces of discipline pay off when I got my college diploma. Once I held that thing in my hand, I knew I had majorly accomplished something, despite the experts taunting me, "You'll never make it," and "You don't deserve that grade." The blessings I have in my life right now are because of my determination and discipline.

Self discipline involves the mastery of oneself. Plato, the great Greek philosopher said, "The first and best victory to conquer is yourself." That was not always the case with me in my college years. I knew I wanted that degree at Texas Tech University. But there were competitive voices: music, video games, and friends. My junior year (during the second semester) I went wild and roomed with a young man my mother disapproved of. True to form, I wasn't able to study much. However, in later years, I buckled down and started cracking open the books. I switched my major three times in my college endeavor. I started with Public Relations, then switched to Broadcast Journalism. Then I found my niche in Political Science minoring in Communication. It was the discipline and the mentoring of students and adults that helped me achieve my degree. A little self-discipline goes a long way.

In "Lessons in Mastery" by Tony Robbins, he introduces a principal that I like. Entrepreneurs wanting quality products and services need discipline. But one principle he drills in is the commitment to constant and never-ending improvement. My Granddad used to tell us, "Accept nothing but the best. Do your best, and the rest will follow." Another thing he taught me is, "If you want something done right, do it yourself." For the last 5 or six years in life, Granddad owned his own brake and alignment shop. He worked long hours to provide for his family, and he taught me principles that last a lifetime, one of which is discipline.

I don't generally use thoughts from movies, but while listening to a Tony Robbins tape, I thought of the movie Karate Kid . At the beginning of Daniel's training Mr. Miagi had him do a variety of chores: "Sand the floor, wax the car (remember wax on wax off?), and paint the fence." One night, Daniel came to him, impatient and frustrated at doing these chores, and asked, "How does it teach me karate?" Mr. Miagi then took Daniel's hands and arms and showed him the karate moves that he had been learning doing all those chores. It's the little daily improvements that make a very well self-disciplined entrepreneur.

Part of a self-disciplined life is meeting our expectations. I had a close business friend of mine 2 decades ago tell me, "Jimmy, you don't get what you want, you get what you expect." You have to examine your expectations and line them up with self-discipline actions and results. It could be in the little things at first. The more disciplined you are, the bigger the expectations will grow. And chances are, bigger victories will come your way.

Part of being self-disciplined as an entrepreneur is the constant ability of your business to solve a problem. Use this as a big take-away moment. If you're not out solving problems that your business claims to solve, then where is the self-discipline? I like to say to people in my daily life: my mother, my associates at the University, my friends at Church, "I solve problems, that's what I do."

Great entrepreneurs must have a competitive edge. And to have this competitive edge, you need some good self-discipline. Let me be authentic here, your competitors don't care that you're only marketing to one small segment. Competitors don't care about the downturn of the economy and how it affects your company. What they will take notice of is when you put yourself in the driver's seat, be self-disciplined, and let that drive you to a competitive edge. Your competitors will go crazy wondering why you are so successful.

To be self disciplined requires courage. "It takes courage to keep going," Les Brown said. I also agree with him when he says it takes courage when you've been knocked down to start again. But if a person wants to be a successful entrepreneur, they must keep going.

I dislike someone calling me a coward, and so I will use that to be disciplined. The reason I hate being called a coward is because my mother's side of the family (her paternal line) comes from a stock of Irish and

Native Americans who weren't afraid to fight if necessary.

Les Brown explains, "If you lose the courage to do what you know has to be done, and you seek the approval of others, then you have lost your nerve."

Remember when I said I was with my ex-wife in a business model? I was gung ho about delivering presentations. But I got sidelined by my ex-wife's critical disapproval of how I made presentations. I didn't let it affect me first. But due to being battered around, I lost my nerve. But now, my nerve is back. I know what has to be done. I have a speaking business to start, books to write, and money to be made. I'm a disabled guy just trying to take care of my mother. So, I, and anybody else in my situation have to get self-disciplined again and get some backbone (courage).

At this writing, I just got through talking to my mother, and she had a wonderful idea. If you want to have strong self-discipline, you need to have a bedrock of faith in God. My faith is the center of everything I do (in Church, family, friends, and business/school). I try to treat people the way the Lord would want others to be treated. Regardless of whether you want to be a successful entrepreneur or a marathon runner, or both, you have to have some faith to keep you disciplined.

Also to be self-disciplined, you need to give the tasks at hand all you have. Les Brown said, "Do more than you are paid for." Although I disagree with Trump's economic policies, the one thing he said in a book he co-authored with Robert Kiyosaki, "You need to go beyond the call of duty." His audience in that particular chapter is to college students. I guess this appealed to me as a postgraduate student myself. My maternal grandfather always instilled in me the value to do my absolute best. That's right, in being self-disciplined, you must strive for excellence.

Les Brown further states, "If you are in a habit of being mediocre, it'll become a part of your consciousness." This goes further into the striving for excellence. I hate the word mediocre. I was labeled that and mentally retarded in school. The state experts for the blind did the same thing when I was going for my degree, but I rose above it and was all I could become at that time. As I said earlier, the true reward for all that self discipline is having the diploma in my home office.

OK, we're nearing the end of the chapter, and I feel I need to go into how these traits are really one. Determination and discipline go hand in hand on one thing. A successful entrepreneur must have a positive mental attitude in order to attain determination and discipline. I agree with Les Brown that you cannot lose your nerve. Let's go back to the college diploma. I was knocked around 2 times, having to change my major three times. The state experts would say, "You're making a mistake. You may not succeed in your career. This degree path is the wrong path." I just ignored it. Why? because I had the positive mental attitude that my knowledge in political science would help me someday, whether I ran for elective office, or chose to be the President and CEO of my own company-or both. I choose the latter. But I had to have the nerve, the positive mental attitude, the faith to attain discipline and determination.

Let me end this on a positive note. I have been knocked down by the storms of life. But I have one anchor that can help me stay determined and self-disciplined. It is my faith. You can have faith in the Universe, the Creator, whoever it may be. My faith is in God, and that anchor of faith is what keeps me going. Determination and discipline rely on faith.

CHAPTER 5 -
PERSONALITY AND CHARACTER

"Integrity fears no hidden cameras." - Brad Wilcox

At this time, the wee hours of the morning, I was watching videos on YouTube when I ran across the above mentioned quote. Yes, we are talking about ethics. I'm going to give it to you straight, if you want to be a successful entrepreneur, build your character. Bring in your own code of ethics or adopt one given by your industry's code of ethics.

Small business management experts Byrd and Megganson define business ethics as " a standard used to judge the rightness or wrongness of a business's behavior." (Mary J Byrd and -Leon C Megganson Small Business Management, an Entrepreneur's Guidebook Seventh edition, McGraw Hill International p. 85). But is there really such thing as business ethics? It is my hope that this chapter may answer the question and any other questions that come to mind.

JP Morgan, when he testified before Congress in 1895, was asked whether he loaned out to businesses solely because of assets. His reply was, "The first thing is character." He went on to say that if character was missing, he wouldn't loan to the person, even if they had all the bonds and assets necessary.

I may have said this in a previous chapter, but you may have all the investment holdings you want and be a billionaire, but if you don't have character and morality, your success is not good. It will go to your head.

Honesty: This is big. In my childhood, I spent almost every weekend at my maternal grandparents' house. I would sit at the table with my Granddad. From the early childhood, I would hear him say, "Now, James, I never want to catch you in a lie. I hate liars worse than thieves." He would say that if you told one lie, you had to tell a whole web of lies just to cover it up. Honesty was ingrained in me at an early age. I think any successful entrepreneur should have this bedrock virtue to be ethical and successful.

As a kid, I would watch the hit TV show Dallas. A quote JR Ewing said was unbelievable, "Once you give up integrity the rest is a piece of cake." Once again, I think about my Granddad. A lot of my ethical values I have came from him and my mother.

Abraham Lincoln said this of integrity, "I am not bound to succeed, but I am bound to live up to the light I have." Now some of you might say, "But Abe Lincoln was a politician, not an entrepreneur." Actually, that is not the case. In my teen years I would check out biographies about Abraham Lincoln. He would work during the day and study law by night. Before long, he formed a partnership and eventually branched out to his law practice. So yes, President Lincoln, before he was President, was an entrepreneur in that light.

Zig Ziglar said, "True performance is revealed through your integrity, and who you are...every day." To me that means that integrity means being true to who you are every day. Recently, I wrote a blog post called "Don't Check Your Faith at the Door." You may choose to ignore what I have to say, but to me faith reveals your character, which brings forth your integrity. I try to be true to myself more than just on Sundays, but every day in my family, in my business dealings, at school, and every part of my life.

Ziglar goes on to define integrity as "a sense of wholeness...consistency." You must be consistent in your standards. In simpler terms, the standards you have in your faith must carry over to the standards you have in business. Be consistent.

Let me give you an example of integrity. L. Tom Perry, whose religious beliefs prohibited any alcohol, was told he had to participate in a cocktail hour in order to conduct business. Perry agreed, but he went to the bartender asking for something to drink that did not look like alcohol. The bartender filled his glass with milk, allowing him to participate in the cocktail hour without violating integrity, and his principles of faith ("The Tradition of a Balanced Righteous Life," L. Tom Perry January 15, 2010 Utah Valley University). My mother told me a similar story about my uncle. He is an accountant for 50 lawyers, and the firm requires a cocktail hour. My uncle, staying true to his integrity and beliefs, drinks a 7 Up at the cocktail hour.

You say, "Jimmy what if I'm not from your faith background, or any faith background?" To me, it's all about your conscience, what it tells you to do. I don't believe that ethics is bound in faith by everybody, and at the beginning of this chapter I assumed I would be writing to most people who have faith. The core what I'm trying to say is be true to your personal beliefs, even if it's just your own conscience and subconscious mind.

Character: I define character as staying consistent and true to who you are. Character for an entrepreneurial leader in their field is also communicating, consistency, potential, and vision for your organization. Remember the story of L. Tom Perry. He wanted to comply with his firm, but he had the character to stand up for his religious beliefs.

I have an old story which shows my character. In June 1989, I was attending summer school at the Texas School for the Blind and Visually Impaired in Austin, TX. One day after school, the lead houseparent gave us a scavenger hunt, dividing us into teams. Halfway through the scavenger hunt, two guys bailed. I turned to the few that stayed and said, "I'm telling you now, we won't give up on this scavenger hunt." We went on to one of the houses where the hunt ended. To seal our place, we called the lead houseparent, stating that we'd completed the hunt. We were also required to tell him the address of the school, which was no problem for me because I memorized their address in filing applications for the school.

Back at the dorm, a female houseparents said, "You who gave up, you should all be ashamed of yourself. The few guys that are finished with the hunt deserve a pizza party." She then restricted the quitters to their dorm room for the rest of the night.

Go forward 13 years, I was attending a church forum. I told the person I didn't have the ticket, so I would buy another one.

"No, Jimmy. You can go in, but I appreciate your honesty." Determination and honesty formed the character of a businessman.

I think of my Granddad. For the 19 years we were with him, he always showed honesty and integrity, building up his character and reputation in his business. Yes, he had character flaws, but most of my memories of my grandfather were good. He was very protective of me. He always told my uncle (born the same year and one week younger than me), "Andy, you look out for James." He made it clear that if kids picked on me, he would deal with them. Granddad was one of the greatest men I've ever known.

Ethical Codes: A person's ethic is the standards that he wishes to abide by in his personal and business life. I think of the owners of Hobby Lobby. When President Obama set up the mandate that businesses must cover insurance on their employees, including abortion and contraceptives, the owners faced opposition against their personal beliefs. They had a legal battle and won. It goes to show you that if you want to be a successful entrepreneur, you must fight for our personal and business standards.

Let's say you're starting a wholesale business selling food products, and say a serious supplier wants you to put organic pork on your shelves. Your personal moral beliefs may be offended, as you favor Kosher foods. So, you stick by your guns even if you lose the big suppliers. The way I see it, you will find other suppliers later.

Now, let's say you're hired by a corporate event to speak, but this client wants you to speak on Sunday, which is against your religious beliefs.

You try to compromise and offer to give a spiritual message. They might get offended and call off the offer. Hopefully, you can get out and find other corporate sponsors who pay you to stick to your ethical guns.

So far I have discussed the traits and characteristics of an ethical entrepreneur. Now I will further expound on my theory on business ethics, to answer the question if there is such things as business ethics.

The topic itself intrigues me. In community college some years back, during an ethics class, the topic came alive. I hear many people who discuss ethics as "Not everything is black and white, ethics involves many shades of gray." Personally, I don't buy it. And your company ethic should not be separate from your own personal moral code. Sure, many professions/industries have a code of ethics. But in my opinion, you might not need a code book to tell you how to act.

You're probably saying, "Jimmy, you're crazy, people should compartmentalize their personal life and their business." My personal opinion is this, we all have free will to act ethically or to act in an unethical way. You can pick your choice, but you cannot pick the consequences of that choice. One wrong choice can affect your business One ethical choice can have you well esteemed by your business team and the community at large.

Here's an example. Let's say you own your own business that gets contract work from the U.S. Defense Department. Key clients may try to get you to fudge the numbers and the facts. You run a tight ship in your business, and you're well respected by your subordinates. Now, let's say you're in a time crunch to meet the government's deadline, and a manager in your firm wants you to cut corners to meet the deadline. You know that this goes against your ethics for quality and integrity. In my opinion, you should do the best you can with the product or service having the highest quality possible. Because if you act unethically, you may lose your government contract, and other customers may think twice about keeping your business.

So, is there a such thing as business ethics? John Maxwell says no. There's only the Golden Rule and your personal moral code for entrepreneurs to follow. In other words, you should not act differently in your personal life as you do in your business dealings.

Over 20 years ago, in one of my classes, I watched the movie called Absence of Malice with Sally Field and Paul Newman.. At the end of the movie, the characters stood before a panel of Judges. The journalist (the character Sally Field played) told the judges that what she did was ethically right. A judge admonished her,. "You may have done what you thought was ethically right, but it was morally wrong." a judge said. In other words, you could go by a certain professional code and what your business partners wanted you to do, but it would be considered morally wrong by society at large.

Moral virtues and responsibility take the day. Your ethics and your morals should be the same. Please don't misunderstand me, I'm not trying to preach this, but it is repugnant, in my opinion, to compartmentalize your professional/business ethics apart from your personal moral code.

Let me give you another example. We have a man that co-owns a family consulting business. There is a intense competition to get ahead. Normally, the man (we'll call him Rich) has the same moral and ethical code. But he wants a set of clients really bad. So he does something unethical to win their business.

Let's say this spills over into his personal life. His wife discovers his behavior is unethical/immoral. It is possible then that she loses trust in her husband. Unfortunately, Rich is bound to this ethical decision to win this competition. His family is torn apart by the competition, and trust is lost. This could be seen as a serious ethical/moral blunder that could sink their company and cause harm to their family.

Let me give this to you straight. Business ethics on their own, do not exist. Your personal ethical and moral code should not be separate from your business. You as an entrepreneur have to take responsibility for your actions. You cannot be unethical in business and at the same time personally have moral virtue. That has the makings of a hypocrite. You cannot also be both personally and corporately unethical, because customers and others will see it, and you will lose business. You have to have the same moral and ethical code, in my opinion, to have the winning personality and be very successful in your business.

I've attended a few business management courses where they teach that business ethics involves blurred lines You know, shades of gray? Well, I don't personally buy it. You can't have the different moral and ethical side you have in public as well as personally. I believe that college and universities teach ethics the wrong way. I believe in a values-based education, whether it is traditional or nontraditional.

Finally, I wish to expand on what is ethics. It's being honest and taking responsibility for your actions. Be accountable and teachable. Follow the rules you set for your company. Be true to yourself, I know that might be painful for those with serious ethical dilemmas. You have to make a moral decision that you can live with.

So is there such thing as business ethics? Not without bringing in your personal moral code. As an answer to the question I've referred at the beginning of this chapter, there is only ethics. If you can follow what I am saying in this chapter, you can become a successful entrepreneur who has this key trait, ethical behavior. The concept of ethical/moral behavior must be grasped.

CHAPTER 6 -
FAITH: WHAT IS IT?
THE ESSENTIALS OF FAITH

"Faith is not passive, it's active." Theologian Charles Stanley

You may be an entrepreneur running a rising startup that is strong and healthy, and that may make you wealthy. But if you push aside faith and humility, you lose everything that matters most. You destroy yourself. I think that people in this world (even myself) have lost sight of what matters most. People are trying to move ahead in this corporate world of madness. I'm not saying there's anything wrong with it. Money is not the root of all evil, it is the love of money that is the root of all evil.

Last week I watched a conference of leaders from my church. The teachings of last weekend's conference seriously convicted me. I felt I had lost sight of good priorities to replace them with superficial things. I am trying to reform, like replacing watching video game missions to watching faith lifting and motivating videos. It's going to take time, but eventually, for any person who wishes to define themselves as successful, faith has to be a part of absolutely everything they do.

I have wonderful people surrounding me, giving me inspiration to improve my career, and my personal life: friends, teachers of faith, my Toastmasters group, mentors, a very supportive sister and brother-in-law, and awesome church family.

Last, but certainly not least, is my beautiful flower of a mother. Everyday, she takes the rough, unrefined, uncivilized me at the beginning of the day and helps me become more refined, civilized, and presentable. She is an unsung hero in my life. She is the first person who taught me to have faith in the Lord. I say this again: I make Him the center of everything I do. Let's look at Dr. Stanley's quote I put at the beginning of the chapter. Also, do you remember discussing determination in Chapter 4? Well, determination and faith go hand in hand. Remember the story on how I got my apartment near my girlfriend at the time. Well, I prayed, I cried out to the Lord, I fasted, and finally the answer came. I'm not saying the Lord answers everything on time, but it requires you to have faith.

You ask, "Jimmy, how does faith make me a better entrepreneur?" You must have faith in something- the Universe, yourself, and my favorite, God. You may be a billionaire with multiple holding companies, but if you lack the faith that gives you morals to govern your life (remember Chapter 5) your success as an entrepreneur means nothing. If you step on people all the way to the top, that's not a moral way of exercising your faith. I say, though, if you don't want to have faith in God, believe in yourself and follow the dictates of your own conscience. But I say again, faith in God helps.

Let me give you a real world example of entrepreneurs who make their faith the center.

A young man got into Princeton, but quickly discovered that college was not his road of learning. He felt he could learn more by working on products and services, so he dropped out. It was tough, he had a wife and a 14-month old son to look after. Life was tough at first. They ended up living in a relative's basement. Yet he held on, and he knew that God would take care of him. His business blossomed. He had three offices in Utah, China, and the main headquarters in San Diego. This, in my opinion, is a successful entrepreneur who through faith set the bar high to achieve his dreams.

Now, I will give you a hypothetical case. Suppose you own a media consulting firm, and you are trying to consult various media to bring out more family-oriented films and series. You have a strong faith in God. But some of the media outlets don't buy into your vision of faith.

So, you need to connect to those CEOs of media that share even the slightest particle of faith that you have. Like kind brings forth like kind. You can better consult with these clients who share even the slightest bit of faith that you do, and it can be successful. You may not make that much money out of it, but you can sleep at night knowing that through your faith, you did the right things.

Remember Chapter 5 on Ethics? Well what I'm about to write shows that faith and ethics(morality) are linked together.

Faith and Ethics

Because of the Enron scandal and the scandal of those who puffed up the housing market until the bubble burst in 2007, it can be hard to find some businesses that would take integrity and character over the bottom line. I have a few though that are notables of our day.

We'll start with David Green, founder of Hobby Lobby. Remember Chapter 5 when the Obama Administration passed the Health and Human Services (HHS) mandates that required businesses to provide insurance that would cover contraception and birth control. Green joined in a class action lawsuit among other businesses to make a faith based business exempt from the HHS mandate. In the end, Green won, and I credit his character for standing up to something that would violate his beliefs.

Then, there's Truett Cathy. He required that all Chick-fil-A stores be closed on Sunday. And when he made a public statement favoring traditional values, protests broke out in front of his stores. However, there were even more people coming to buy his product because of his stance. Cathy is well known for helping train leaders to have integrity and adding value to others in America.

Last but not least, I look at the life of Heber J Grant. His character started at home. His mother, Rachel's, family told her that they would take care of her and her child if she would abandon her faith and move back into the family fold. Despite the financial struggle, Rachel refused to renounce her faith, and though they struggled, this example added to Heber's character and integrity and made him the man as he was for his time.

Faith is the answer, a key trait of successful entrepreneurs, a concept a good self-made man or woman must grasp. But what is the question? Beyond personal concerns, an entrepreneur taking a macro approach might ask, "Why did a competitor's business succeed, but mine is failing?" or "Why is it that suppliers want me to sacrifice what I believe, but these people could give serious cash?" My answer is faith-faith that while you are being tested in your business, you can succeed the tests by the trial of your faith.

OK, I will give other examples of businessmen of faith that slogged on through adversity. After this, you can read Chapter 10 on adversity.

Faith and Adversity

We all may know some famous businessmen who held to their faith principles in adversity: David Green (Hobby Lobby), Henry Heinz (Heinz Corporation), and Truett Cathy (Chick Fil-A). All entrepreneurs must wade through adversity.

A few years ago, a speech I was supposed to make fell through. Though it hit me hard, I decided to fulfill the blessing of becoming an author. Then the inspiration of my blog came forth.

There is an adage in my faith that goes like this. "Faith is knowing that good will come no matter what happens to us." I believe this is a simple answer. My belief is faith is hoping in things unseen that are true.

OK, let me give you an example in the business world, a hypothetical if you will. Suppose you run a family advertising business, with each partner working profit sharing. Now, you agreed that the firm will not work on Sunday, allowing the leaders and the staff to take a day off. One of your partners wants to work the business that day to attract clients who want to buy on Sunday. You're the President of the Company. The wise thing to do is stick to the requirements of your faith by not working on Sunday; to attend worship services, to spend close quality time with your families. This may cost money, and it might make the partner who wants to work on Sunday bail and find his own business. You may lose money, but faith creates the difference, and you can probably work more efficiently this way anyway.

Now let me give you another hypothetical example. Suppose you own a public relations firm that does some political consulting as well. But one of your clients want the PR to cover a pro-choice abortion group, which is against your faith. What must you do? To be understood, I would recommend that client to a PR firm that might be more friendly to their cause. But I would not sacrifice my faith and morals just to make serious money.

Now I will give you a real world example that is more positive. I saw a video on Youtube where a woman juggles, faith, business, family, plus partners with her husband's organization. She believes that, "You can hold to your faith while maximizing your profits."

I wear many hats in my life at this point. I was attending University studying Communication and Management classes, I'm an author, an elder in my church, plus I take care of my mother. After attending several conferences and listening to tapes in the mid to late 1990's, I've discovered development must go like this: Faith in God first, family second, and your calling as an entrepreneur third. It is a principle that I can embrace and buy into.

Remember the story that I wrote in Chapter 4? I would like to expound on this. I didn't receive my degree at Texas Tech University through discipline and determination alone. It was my faith that helped me endure the naysaying "experts" who were not interested in my success! I had faith in God that He would help me pursue my career. I did not end up in law school as I originally planned, but now I am called of God to motivate people in temporal as well as in spiritual matters.

Now, lastly, I must discuss the opposite of faith, which is fear. More than ten years ago, I was starting my second chance in business. An associate of mine said, "Fear is False Evidence Appearing Real." At first, I thought it was a statement he heard from church. But about two years ago, I saw a talk by Robert Kiyosaki and learned that he had coined the statement. You overcome fear with faith. Like perfect love casts out fear (1 John 4:18), so does exercising a particle of your faith. Then, and only then, will you face and overcome the challenges known as fear.

Remember the apartment story from earlier? Well, after fasting, pleading, and praying, the Lord gave me an answer to not give up. My parents felt like the odds were stacked against me. While they went to talk to management, being tempted to lose faith, I told myself that greater is my faith than that fear. Don't fail out of fear; find faith that will sustain you. I know it's not easy, and some of you probably glossed over this chapter because you felt it didn't apply to you. Let me tell you something, faith overcomes fear of rejection and fear of failure!

I'm not going to sugar-coat the end of this chapter. I have been in circumstances of darkness, and at some point, my faith faltered. But over a period of 5 years, I realized that my faith was tested. You may face business reversals, even bankruptcy. But have faith, hold on to your dreams.

I will finally conclude with a personal example which was a test of my faith. In January 2018, I planned to launch my business full-time. I was on top of the word. I was writing a speech which was to be my debut speech on my Christian theory of the Law of Attraction. The night before the speech, I was having dinner at my nephew's house. I was getting ready to go home. It was very dark except a lone porch light, and being legally blind, I could barely see. I swore I was stepping onto the stairs when I fell off the porch and broke my leg!

For 18 hours, except for surgery prep and recovery room time, I was scared out of my mind! Everything in my life was put on hold. After surgery, I was taken to rehabilitation facility. I spent two months there recovering at the rehab center, where I also contracted pneumonia. I almost wanted to give up. It was my faith and hope that pushed me through.

CHAPTER 7 -

LIFE AND CHANGE DO CALL FOR SETTING GOALS

"A winner doesn't quit...A winner keeps his eye on the goal." Dexter Yeager.

You may ask, "Jimmy, how can change help you set goals?" Sometimes your circumstances change, and you will need to set different goals. If you remember Chapter 6, you can't set and meet goals without faith.

At this writing it is Easter Sunday afternoon. In Church, we talked about Christ's atonement, our imperfectness, and the grace, the enabling power to make changes.

Dexter Yeager's quote makes me think of an old adage I heard about in high school, "Keep your eyes on the prize." This is a secret every entrepreneur, any trailblazer, and pioneer in an industry is to see the beginning of the end in mind.

Let me tell you my goals and aspirations. I would like to be a best-selling author, motivational speaker, and maybe do some PR media consulting on the side. I hope to be so financially solvent that I can go into another business model (another network marketing business).

Now I want you to do something so you're still with me. Close the book, set a bookmark in your place, and for 20 minutes write down your goals. Be specific.

Please seriously take the 20 minutes to think and reflect about this. If you don't, I promise you, you're cheating yourself. If you do the exercise, you'll come back learning more content and have a stronger resolve to achieve your goals.

All right, I hope you took the time to write your goals and aspirations. IF you did that, congratulations, I can take you through goals and then on to the characteristics of networking, service, and adversity. But let's get back to learning about goals.

If you didn't do the challenge, there's a rebel inside of you. Nonetheless, some entrepreneurs are non-conformists, so there's hope for you.

I can bet your passion keeps you awake at night. It gnaws in your spirit to start your dreams. To be secure, you must do the challenge. Jim Rohn said that if we make a written list of goals, that our income and profits would skyrocket.

A therapist I saw 20 years ago suggested that goals could be founded in concrete, but they should be allowed to move in sand. I've been counseled to be patient and celebrate the little victories when you have accomplished a goal.

You make New Year's resolutions to make changes in your life. Remember discipline in Chapter 4? The reason most people don't see their goals through is because they may be good people who lack discipline.

On the road to success, our goals, great or small cannot be achieved without discipline and determination.

You must have written goals. Delatorro McNeal said that "Goals takes the situation in life and...using laser beam focus on what we want in life."

At a conference I attended nearly four years ago, I learned that the only way to achieve goals is to "write it down." Habakkuk says, "Write the vision, make it plain." (Habakkuk 2:2, KJV)

McNeal goes on to say that the top 3% of successful people have written goals. The top 3% of entrepreneurs have written their goals and work toward achieving them. That means 97% of people must work for the top 3%. Achieving goals should follow with awesome rewards. Rewards like, "If I sell two cases of laptops, we'll go out to eat at a high end restaurant," or, "If I sell 5 accounts of my dog grooming service, we'll go to Hawaii." The list of awesome rewards can go on and on as you achieve written goals.

There are some problems that even the most intuitive entrepreneurs have with goals. Zig Ziglar said that the problem is that "Most people are not raised that way, and our educational system has not taught people that setting goals is necessary to do." In my eyes, setting goals should be a life skill, a lifetime principle.

Ziglar also assessed some other problems in getting people to set goals, "They fear ridicule, someone telling them they can't achieve the goal...and they have not met anyone who has achieved any major goals." I see this in my life as well as in other people's lives. I used to be ridiculed by people saying I would never graduate from high school, never go to and graduate from college. Well, I proved them wrong. Even with that though, if I've been ridiculed once, I need at least ten positive motivations for every one time I have been shot down, so I see Zig Ziglar's assessment on goal problems is very correct.

If we're going to achieve our goals, we have to find ways to rise above the ridicule, even limit exposure to some people who would ridicule you or waste your time. I am having to learn this lesson the hard way. Some friends are not as involved in my life, and some have left my life because of where I stand on my goals.

Ziglar suggests that people make a list of goals, "and see if you can write one simple sentence. Then, you narrow it down on what you absolutely want to achieve. You must know that you need help to achieve your goals."

Don't waste your time with senseless chatter, idleness, and gossip. Follow the plan for your goals, and eliminate interruptions.. Gossip, criticizing, and drama have no place for the person who has a goal-centered

life. After all, goal-setting is a process.

Not wasting time helps you move with purpose, and it becomes easier to achieve your goals, which leads to higher motivation and effectiveness.

November and December are times when I set my goals. Isn't it sad how almost everybody abandons their goals by March. It's because they didn't have the strong resolve and reasons to do it.

Let me give you a hypothetical example. Brian owns a paint service business. He has a goal of waking up early to a more positive morning routine. So he wakes up at 5:30, jogs 10 laps around his yard, and goes inside for a healthy breakfast: a health bar, or some hard boiled eggs, or some whole wheat toast with peanut butter. He arrives at the office/warehouse an hour before his employees are there. While listening to a motivational CD, he checks his inventory, and gives notes of constructive criticism to the young man that keeps track of his inventory. In the morning, he meets with prospective clients and customers. He stays in for lunch, perhaps eating a chicken salad sandwich. In the afternoon, he drives to a worksite to check on and supervise the painters in his employ. He makes a notation for the man who was late for work, and another one for a man falling asleep on the job. He has a goal for quality employees. They are given two warnings for undesirable activity at work. Then, if he pleases, he can use employment at will and fire them. He is a man of goals, and while he treats his employees well and adds value to them, he does not tolerate substandard work or problems with punctuality. He's the go-getter in that neighborhood of businesses.

Now let's look at his routine at home. He gets home from work, reads a positive book, and when the kids gets home, he plays with them for a little while. At dinner, he asks his wife and kids how their days went. He would then instill in his kids the values he had for his business. He assigns the older kids chores and pays them an allowance. Once the child is 7 or older, he will have them taken to his paint shop and office and teach them to do odd jobs for the business.

Let's give another hypothetical example. Sarah desires multiple income streams. So she sets up three businesses. The one she first started was a law firm, she being a very shrewd and skilled lawyer. She also co-owns a public relations firm, making her husband the CEO of that firm, which he has along with his educational products sold on the Internet. The couple also has a network marketing business. The law firm gives her a net worth of $1,200,000. The PR firm gives both each a net worth of $87,000. The network marketing firm gives them $140,000 which she splits with her husband.

When they take time for home and family, her husband sets the chores for their two teenage sons and two teenage daughters. Though they have plenty, they choose to live in a modest town home. As people of faith, they don't want their affluence to ruin their values they pass on to their children. Business takes a lot of their time, but Sarah and Will, decide when to take a break and focus more on home and family.

Now I give you yet another hypothetical example. Ashley co-owns an advertising firm. Her goal is to provide a nest egg for her and her three children. A widow of 2 months, Ashley works hard for those kids. She makes a net worth of $1,000 weekly with her advertising firm a stipend paid by her father. But she is being pressured by a friend to sell him her business. He could offer her $10,000 down for the business and make payments of $230,000 a month for the business. Ms. Cooper is tempted, but her friends on the board believes if she sold the firm, it would go belly up, with no residual income for her and the children.

<u>My Goals</u>

In the past, I have encountered obstacles in regard to achieving my goals. I let a personal matter, or several of those, interfere with my networking goals, and my network marketing business failed as a result. But I still have goals. I'm not giving up.

One of my goals is to get my name out there as a motivational speaker. I would like to deliver speeches to colleges and universities, including my alma mater, as well as at corporate events. My speeches would be about overcoming adversity as well as being an entrepreneur. Why do I have these goals? What is my motivation? I have a mother I promised I would never leave, and that I would take care of her. I want to leave a legacy for my nieces and nephews, adopted or bloodline, so they can reap the benefits of my calling, my dream.

Research and Goal- Setting Theory

George and Jones, mentioned earlier in the book, made plain the issue of goal setting theory. "Goal setting theory is the process of motivating workers to do their jobs and meet organizational goals" (George & Jones p. 310). The researchers went on to discuss the criteria for setting goals as a proving ground for this theory.

1. Be Specific : The authors state this as a main criteria for setting goals. Motivational speakers and others in the business and personal development worlds have clearly stated that your goal must be written down and specific. Most of them in those would recommend putting these goals and what you want on a mirror or refrigerator door, and reading the goals every morning as you start your day.

2. Raising standards: Tony Robbins and I agree on this part. Part of working to accomplish your goal is that it must have a higher standard and priority above leisure. I firmly believe that it is time for me to raise my standards. At middle age, I don't want to waste any more time on frivolous things. I need people who will help me succeed.

Think about this, you wake up in the morning and get dressed. You look at your goals, but you discern there will be obstacles. Your significant other is demanding and wants more time with you. Don't let a person like this destroy your dream. So what do you do? You have a lunch date instead with a friend who has ideas to help you start and work your business. Simply put, you raise your standards. Balancing business and family together is a hard thing, but if you raise your standards, you can still see your significant other, and they can give you ideas to help your dream. However, if the relationship is toxic to your goals (if unmarried) you get out of that relationship as soon as you can.

Now, let's think of another situation. You wake up one morning, get dressed and look over your goals. You were up and down all night, and you don't feel so well. However, you know that a supplier wants to meet with you and your managers to give suggestions about a marketing strategy. It's a home business, but your supplier wants to meet you near his business. Your goal for the day is to get more inventory as well as brainstorming for effective advertising techniques. You decide to go because that supplier is important to you and your company goals.

I hope that I have given you something to chew on when it comes to goals. Remember this, don't give up. If you don't give up, and if you keep your eye on the goals you want to achieve, you will make it as a successful entrepreneur.

CHAPTER 8 -
BUSINESS NEEDS NETWORKING

"Network like it's going out of style." -Delatorro McNeal

This evening at this writing (April 10, 2015), I had a chance to attend UT Permian Basin's Students in Free Enterprise (SIFE- hereafter Enactus) meeting. Professor Crain greeted me before the meeting, and as it started, he gave his insights that he hoped we students would have the entrepreneurial spirit enough to join with him in owning a business model. One of those is an online art store where artists sell their paintings. We also discussed the 2015 Entrepreneurial Expo at UTPB. I had the opportunity to introduce a local radio marketing director, thus linking entrepreneurship and communication. I also nominated myself to be Project Manager for SIFE for the next year, elected unanimously under endorsement by the leadership. And with that, I left the meetings.

Let me give you some insights I've gained from Enactus. An ambivert entrepreneur must have foresight to work with a team to design an effective business model, or buy into a system that has a working business model. This may involve being trained by mentors who were trail-blazers themselves. Dr. Mike Murdock, a pastor and wisdom-trainer says, "You can either mistake your way through life or mentor your way through life." You need a mentor and a mastermind group if you hope to be a successful entrepreneur.

The winning personality must also have the dedication and determination to step up to the plate. I saw this in my first Enactus meeting. There were those who sat on the sidelines, and there were those who stepped in and took initiative.

The winning personality must also have good ties to family and faith. I sure do thank my mother for picking me up from that first Enactus meeting and allowing me to come. I also thank her for helping me get things together for the meeting. As I said, she takes the rough, unrefined, uncivilized me at the beginning of the day and helps me become more refined, civilized, and presentable. I thank God for my Mama.

Faith is another thing I had also mentioned. I'd like to consider myself as devout, principled, dependable, raised with conservative values and values of the entrepreneurial spirit. This country needs entrepreneurs and leaders of faith to step up to the plate and instill the values America needs.

Seriously, network and find yourself with a mentor or two. They can give you life lessons to help you succeed in your field of business. I have had quite a few mentors in life, but the important part of mentoring and networking is good listening.

In 2016, after consulting with family and friends, I decided that Spring 2016 was to be my last semester at the University. I went to the faculty advisor to discuss my reasons for leaving.

"One reason I'm leaving is because not very many people are researching public speaking, motivation, and leadership," I said to him.

"Well be a trail-blazer, Jimmy. You can do it." He said.

"I'll stay in touch," I replied.

"You'd better," he said with a smile.

As my business grows, I will partner with Enactus. They've given me the networking skills to branch out into my business and branding. Yes, that's right, networking can bring in people that can help enhance your brand and help it be consistent When I was in network marketing, I would go to their various business conventions. I networked with a variety of people. Some gave me pearls of wisdom. Some gave me pointers. At the time, I was dating, engaged to, and married to my ex-wife. While the learning and networking parts of the convention were taking place, I was excited. I came alive. My ex-wife however, was not, and I believe that is part of what hurt our business.

Research suggests that there are five tips for networking entrepreneurs. I will go through them one at a time, however I have made a few changes from my perspective.

1. Get connected with social media. I can't stress this enough. Some suggest Twitter, but if you want my perspective, go with Facebook and LinkedIn. Through networking and learning opportunities there, you might be able to sell your product or your branding, and your business could (though there are no guarantees) be on its way up to the top.

In Caught Between a Dream and a Job, Delatorro McNeal advises developing a Web presence. "Have a presence on Social media such as Youtube...or Facebook." I have a Facebook page for my brand and my company, as well as a youtube channel, podcast, and a blog. Back to LinkedIn, seriously check into that one more than the others because of the networking opportunities to sell your brand, product, or services. Why just today, I checked my LinkedIn page. My uncle, who is an accountant shared some tips in the accounting field. You can use your social networking platforms to market your brand/product/service. The other networking tips will help you get ideas on how to do your marketing.

2. Get with and join a local networking organization for entrepreneurs. Top authors and businessmen Robert Kiyosaki and Donald Trump say it best, and I emphasize this myself. Get with like-minded people. They have local Cashflow Clubs in almost all cities. Also look in the newspaper or online for networking groups. If you're a student, I strongly advise joining Enactus, and if you're an entrepreneur, Enactus needs you as a partner. If you're an aspiring speaker, by all means, join Toastmasters.

To me, social networking online is a soft science in entrepreneurship. This is where the real marketing and networking starts.

For starters, I met my brother-in-law in a leadership class almost 8 years ago, before he met my sister. Now I have a link to his family business Facebook page. I've told him that if he wanted me to do some marketing for him, I would. But back to networking, network marketing is a good tool. I strongly advise investing in it (Don't knock it till you really tried it).

Once you find this group, go to seminars and conferences where you link up with like-minded people in your industry who can give you pointers, or invest and buy into the business you have. Get into industry-related networking opportunities. If you want to be a part of leadership in your industry of entrepreneurs, networking on a local basis is key. If there isn't anything local, find another one close by. And like the quote of Delatorro McNeal says, "Network like it's going out of style."

The people you network with can give you tips on how to run, manage, and market your business. They can invest into your idea and help you be an expert in the industry you wish to be a part of. With all my years observing others in business, I have noticed that networking has often given entrepreneurs the tips, investment, and confidence to start and launch their business, bring out advertising and marketing techniques.

My senior year in high school, I considered studying Political Science, through the coursework there at Texas Tech University. I learned there that no leader is an island. Also, I learned the basics of the art of networking. I've turned back from being a politician and chose instead to work in the private sector. I want now to be a leader and motivator.

But let me inform you this, if you don't network, if you go stealth, you are not a real leader and your business is going to fail.

3. Don't be afraid to ask for connections. Now consider this, if you network with a good organization, you need a mentor and meet potential partners. Let your mentor help you, and find fellowship with potential partners. Ask for connections that can help your product, service, or brand grow. Don't think to yourself, "I can't do it because my friends say I'm crazy

for branching out." Who's going to help you run your business? Your family? Your friends? None of them will unless they rally behind you and see your value of networking to receive connections.

4. Organize a local meet up. Arrange to meet and discuss business with a local mentor, or a mentor who is close by. You'll get the gist of their values as well as their companies' values.

An entrepreneur who plans to build and grow his business should have a coach or mentor. They can set you up with connections with leaders on a regional scale who can mentor your business and life in a favorable light. Connect yourself with local leaders who can put you in a favorable business model. Seize the opportunities that local leaders in your industry urge you to take.

5. Set up contact with local media

If you have low or no budget, I highly recommend you contact local media. If you don't know how to write a press release, look it up on search engines or search videos. If it's not your forte, get someone acquainted with media to help you reach the most audiences and help you further your networking and connections.

You should not be afraid of asking for connections. This is your baby, your business to manage and grow. These connections will help you with your company, maybe a life coach will come out of it, because you're going to need it in your business to work hard.

In 2012, I opened my third bid for a business. My friend took me to a halfway meet up with a mentor who lived 3 hours away. My friend, who was not too interested in the industry went inside the restaurant, while we met outside to talk business and help authorize the deal.

Whether you are a new entrepreneur or a veteran. Either way, public relations is an excellent way to market your product. PR can be a useful marketing strategy to test a way to drive traffic of commercials to a business.

Another networking tool is this: volunteering. You may say, "How in the world, Jimmy can my business launch and grow by volunteering?" It's because if you do volunteering for a cause you believe in, you'll send your business into a catapult launch. For those of you devout in your faith, there's plenty of service opportunities there. You may want to join service organizations like Toastmasters and the Lions Club (to name a few). I mention this because Toastmaster helps me sharpen my speaking skills. Through the Lions Club, I was sent a few years to their wonderful summer camp. In my personal belief, service opportunities are the best place to network.

Here are a few more tips:

Pretend this is you and me in a conversation where you get a cup of coffee (or beverage of choice). Over a beverage, I've seen mentors give a pep talk encouraging people to do their best to succeed.

Get in touch with your Small Business Development Center (SBDC) on your local college campus. There's plenty of resources for networking, so we don't have an excuse to network with people that can help your business grow, even bringing we have no excuse not to network.

CHAPTER 9 -
A WINNING PERSONALITY SERVES

"When you are in the service of your fellow beings, ye are also in the service of your God." - The Book of Mormon

For this discussion, I'm going to wax a wee bit political. After all, my first Bachelor's degree was in Political Science. I will analyze a phrase in President John F. Kennedy's Inaugural Address. I want to talk about his appeal to public service, and I will use it to prepare entrepreneurs to have a servant's heart to collaborate for the good around them. Kennedy clearly states in his Inaugural Address, "And so my fellow Americans, ask not what your country can do for you. Ask what you can do for your country."

The winning personality must have a servant's heart. President Kennedy saw the need for service when the country was locked in the Cold War. He founded the Peace Corps, and young people who liked his message signed up to do service with them. Because of this, when I was an undergraduate student at Texas Tech University, President Clinton formed Americorp, a semi-service job for college students.

For as long as I remember, I wanted to be the first blind President of the United States. Politics was a common discussion at my Granddad's table. We talked about politics, history, faith in God, and business. But this is a book for entrepreneurs, not politicians. Should my business income someday reach to the millions, I plan to set up service for a cane bank for blind people who don't have a state agency to pay for a specialized cane. An entrepreneur with a winning personality should keep service in their heart, and kick arrogance to the curb.

Let me tell you a story about the need for service. It was a cold sunny morning when my ex-wife and I were in a van full of prospective entrepreneurs. One of the ladies had listened to my ex-wife's conversation. "If you want your business to succeed, you have to give and serve," she said with prudence in her eyes.

"But maybe I don't want to give and serve," My ex-wife protested. As a result, our support in the business crumbled. My ex-wife and I argued about how the business should be. Finally, she gave it up. Nine months later, we separated, and she filed for divorce. Had she hung in there and took those associates' advice to heart, we might have succeeded. All this stuff on serving, I wouldn't ask you to do this if I wasn't willing to do it myself.

I'll give you a fictional example. Let's say you own a large software company. You may interview clients in your corner office. But every so often you make yourself accessible to staff and clients. You stop by the cubicles of employees, and instead of chewing them out, you give them constructive criticism, helping them out with what they need.

I think of the Kennedy family. The patriarch, Joseph P. Kennedy Sr. amassed a great fortune. But he and his wife Rose would not tolerate their kids to be lackadaisical. After World War II, John F. Kennedy ran for Congress. The rest is history.

"Jimmy, why would you mention this to me?" you might say. Because I think entrepreneurs should give back to the community, region and nation, to those in need and to assume leadership positions.

I think again of my maternal grandfather. Granddad was the one who gave me the entrepreneurial spirit. One time when I was 15, a telethon was on. Granddad told Grandma that he and his company would match certain gifts to the charity. Whether it happened, I don't know. What I do know is Granddad gave me the servant's heart.

Let me give you a story that happened in my childhood. I was 12, and very interested in the legend of King Arthur and the Knights of the Round Table. I pretended to be a king of the North Province. My uncle

Andy, who was born the same year as I was, engaged me in a dialogue.

"I want to wage war against your province," Uncle Andy said.

"I am a King, get my servants to do those things," I said.

Andy replied emphatically, "All kings go out to battle."

We battled with all our might. But Uncle Andy taught me a valuable lesson. If you want to be a leader in your field, you have to go down where your organization's labor is in order to serve.

Remember the chapter on leadership? Well, I'll give it to you plain. Entrepreneurs can't serve all the needs of their organization. He or she must delegate in order to not have too many irons in the fire. In the early 90's I served as a Secretary, Vice President, and President in different college clubs. I bit off more than I could chew and ended up sick. Under pressure from people I used to call "friends," I resigned as President of one of the organizations. I soon learned that the group was taken over by another club. Within a few weeks after resignation, I also withdrew my membership.

My first year in college, Mother worked for the Food Service Department for the local school district. She would take me to the meetings, which she was President of at the time. In addition to working and taking home paperwork, she did service on the side, and even took a night course in college. I believe that Mama has a servant's heart.

I think a good business model must add value by serving its customers. Best-selling author and economist Paul Zane Pilzer states, "I do business with people for products I wouldn't normally find on the internet...that may cost more...because they add value."

I will give you a hypothetical example of how a company changed a policy of one of its workers toward a client. An insurance company received a claim for a damaged car. Pictures were taken and then lost. The worker's negligent actions led to the loss of the photos. Now suppose I was an entrepreneur in charge of that company, and the mountain of complaints reached my desk. What would I as an entrepreneur do about the damaged relations between a client and an employee?

The customer is always right!, If I saw a pattern, the employee would be terminated promptly, and the claim would be brought over to a manager who would hopefully expedite the claim. What good is a company or an entrepreneur's word if the company does not value its clients?

I have another story. One recent Sunday morning, while picking me up from church, a friend and fellow entrepreneur saw on my property some limbs that a previous West Texas storm had damaged. He volunteered to help clean them up, even though I gave no invitation. That didn't matter. Early one morning, my mother and I arrived on our front porch to find him, his wife, and his kids picking up limbs and putting them in a pile to be hauled away. Their selfless act of service made a major impression on my my mother and me.

Let's say you're a CEO of a family business. You want to make a profit and bring the company to new heights it never has materialized. But let me be point blank, if all you care about is the bottom line without service, prepare for the undertow of potential clients, customers, and employees.

When I think of this, I think of a good friend of mine in Anson, Texas. He's an aspiring minister and evangelist. My friend left school in the 8th grade and attended several years of seminary before receiving a certificate making him an Episcopal Priest with all the rights and privileges thereto. He gives me hope for my career when I stand in judgement of whether my career adds any value to the world.

Perhaps I should give you more nuts and bolts of what service is made of for the entrepreneur.

1. Value your customers and clients. Go the extra mile when serving them. Treat each client or customer equally. The motive for serving them does not always have to be for earning money. Involve the best people

in your organization in serving these clients and customers. The most successful entrepreneurs aren't lone wolves. I agree with a team approach, especially when dealing with your customer base.

2. Serve Your Employees: Help them to make the changes that would benefit the company and its services. However, make sure that they add value to the company too. When serving employees, check out the ones with the most potential who are struggling. Give them encouragement. Don't use the corner office as a soap box to preach your brand of productivity and synergy. If you do that, you may anger employees and push them out of the company

3. Public Service: The best businesses are involved in community service. It's important for businesses to serve the public to be informed on the best possible policies; whether it is on a local, state, or national government. A good businessman will want to serve his community and his country.

4. Value Your Fellow Beings: This is core, the very beginning. If an entrepreneur is too focused on the bottom line, the public image of his or her company may be damaged.

Now I know some of you would say, "OK, there, Jimmy. You're into political science, how does an entrepreneur need to be involved in public service, and why?"

I had a leadership teacher over five years ago tell the class, "If you go to community meetings, you can find out what regulations the community may have The same goes for state and national government.

Years ago, during a brief stint in graduate school, I mentioned one night in class that media businesses needed to be involved in public service to further their public interest. My suggestion was very controversial with my classmates, but I believe my professor agreed with my comments.

If you're an entrepreneur, you need to keep up with current events and do some public service to influence the powers that be to the best interest of the people they serve and the business world.

Twelve years ago, an old friend called me upset because she felt that God hadn't given her a place where He could use her. I suggested that she look around herself for opportunities to serve. I pointed out to her that when you serve your fellow beings, you are serving God. You have to see the need where service is needed. Open doors for people. Say some kind words to those who are struggling. Bless those around you who are suffering.

You say, "Jimmy, you're getting preachy." Well I say this, if I'm preachy, I'm preaching to myself as well. Over ten years ago, I was having deep problems in my social life. When I wasn't out visiting with friends, I was melancholy, lying on my couch feeling sorry for myself. Then one night, a friend from church showed up unannounced.

"Get up, Jimmy," he said. "We gotta help someone move."

We went to this couple's apartment, and I took I don't know how many boxes upstairs. When I was done, I was tired. I didn't feel sorry for myself anymore. Service drives pity out.

At this point, you may be asking, "Jimmy, why should I care?" I said it at the beginning of this book, and I mean it now. If you're a successful billionaire entrepreneur who puts out that he or she don't care, exhibits poor leadership skills to lord over staff and potential clients, uses creativity for one-upmanship in a cut throat business model, uses discipline and determination to step over others as you wrongfully take the lead, if you have bad ethics and no faith, if you further your goals by stepping on others and dealing with heavy-handed authority, ripping off staff and clients, if the entrepreneurs and other people you network with say you make them feel scared, nervous or angry, you got a serious problem!

I mean it, if you don't serve and act like you don't care about your fellow man, plus if you put a price tag on your fellow man, then you are unlikely to hold the winning personality.

CHAPTER 10 -
ADVERSITY TO GO!

Afflictions: everybody has some. Grief, heartache, loneliness, anxiety, disappointments, tribulations. I am no stranger to adversity. Recently, I read out of John 16, verse 33 which says, "In the world ye shall have tribulation, but be of good cheer, I have overcome the world!"

In May 2015, my mother was hospitalized. We came very close to losing her but I held to my beliefs that she would be OK. She had the fighting spirit, and was able to start the recovery process quickly.

Then in February 2016, the howling winds of adversity hit my household again. I will not go into the particulars of how it all began. Suffice it to say that Mama's post surgery depression got worse, and her health dropped some. I spent 1 1/2 months at my mother's house. Sometimes at night, she'd call me to give her a blessing or to solve a health problem to the best of my ability.

I sought wise counsel from friends in Church. I even went to the Temple of the Church of Jesus Christ of Latter-day Saints in Lubbock, Texas, to pray and receive guidance and revelation. On top of the family situation, I had broken off a relationship from a girlfriend, a relationship which I thought had promise. It turned out that her standards and maturity were far below what I wanted in a companion.

But adversity has been a good teacher. Adversity can be a motivator if necessary; the carrot and the stick effect so to speak. I'm a firm believer in positive motivation, but sometimes adversity gives you enough lift to catapult you into your destiny.

Today, I went to a baptism in my Church. One of my fellow elders talked to the audience about "enduring it well." That involves staying close to God, and doing what He tells you according to the dictates of your own conscience. Sometimes afflictions happen because of the free will of others. But remember, we must pass the valleys of adversity to find joy and peace.

Another help is enduring by hanging on to what you know to be true that has a solid foundation. I have written and made speeches on this topic. I believe also to endure well, you must understand that adversity comes in as a boon to catapult you in a position to step into your destiny. Enduring it well means accepting your adversity as a teacher with lessons only time can yield.

You're probably are thinking, "Jimmy I've read almost 2 pages in this chapter, and I have not found a thing about adversity for business and how to overcome it." Well then, let me elaborate.

We all may know some famous businessmen who held to their faith principles in adversity: David Green (Hobby Lobby), Henry Heinz (Heinz Corporation), and Truett Cathy (Chick Fil-A.) I have personally known some businessmen of faith who have also weathered the storm of adversity. All entrepreneurs must wade through adversity.

I have seen this in my life. In 2015, a speech I was supposed to make fell through. Though it hit me hard, I decided to change direction. Thus, the inspiration of my blog came forth.

When I think of good thinkers of faith, I think of William Bradford, the leader of the Pilgrims. He led his people through months of adversity, and pioneered good relations with the Indians, and after one year of being settled in Plymouth, he and his people praised God with a feast to commemorate their overcoming adversity and settling into the new world.

In the book The Many Facets of Leadership , written by Albert Vicare and various authors, one statement stood out to me: "As there is pain in truth, so there is truth in pain." I have seen this principle working time and time again. I came back from a vacation once determined to hit the ground running, but illness struck me down. With the right medication and an inner determination given to me by God, I rose out of my adversity, recovered from my illness.

I will tell you my story on how I overcame some adversities when I was young. I was born legally blind with multiple birth defects. The doctors sat my parents down and said, "He has some characteristics of a mongoloid child, and may not live long." God had other plans; I am not only surviving, but thriving in my health in spite of my birth defects.

When I was 4, an eye doctor sat my mother down and said, "He is non-educatable, there's no hope of a normal education." For three years, I was placed in what would now be a pre-kindergarten program for special needs kids. However, when a vision resource teacher discovered me, and fought for my right to have a normal education, and after going through various specialists, I was able to begin kindergarten in 1978 when I was eight years old.

The label of "slow learner" hung over me. In fifth grade, I was having personal and school problems. However, in the sixth grade, very early in the fall, my teacher drew me aside. What she did, which I thought was tough when I was a kid, made me a better person.

"James, you look me in the eye when I'm talking to you. You are not a slow learner, don't even think that. You will pass this class, and I expect you to pull your weight in this class." I passed the sixth grade and went on through to graduate from high school.

The fall of my senior year of high school brought on a plethora of experts along with a caseworker for the blind in Texas. The mantra was, "James is socially, mentally, and emotionally immature, and he is not fit for college." However, with the help of a few friends from the National Federation of the Blind, I fought for my rights to a college education.

It took seven years of adversity to graduate from college with my first Bachelors degree. There were times I thought about quitting. But I had good cheerleaders, my mother and my maternal grandmother, two maternal uncles, and the woman who would later become my ex-wife.

While in college, I attended several business motivational conferences, seminars, and conventions. Though I wanted a career in law, a seed was planted for me to be someday on stage to inspire, impact, and motivate business and public leaders .

This is a warning- a fledgeling entrepreneur with the winning personality must be careful not to cause their own adversity by having a bad employee ruin the company image. Remember the hypothetical situation of the car insurance claim in chapter 9? Ok, suppose the person is fired. A good PR move might be to sugar coat and tell customers who once had her as their insurance claim person that they have left to pursue other opportunities. Don't make it obvious as to why you terminated them, because such blatant action could cost your company image, lose customers, and a business reversal that causes your own adversity.

In a recent article in Entrepreneur , writer Steve Tobay had these insights to share: "The way you handle adversity, challenge, and competition plays an enormous role in determining how things turn out for you in life. If you try to avoid those factors I guarantee you won't be happy about the outcome. The business world will chew you up and spit you out. Sorry to be so blunt, but that is the truth."

I recall an in the 1980's coaches would tell their athletes, "Remember, no pain no gain." I remember my maternal grandfather poured in blood, sweat, and tears into his car repair business. He came to work early and didn't leave until late in the evening. It was overwhelming on days when he was swamped at work. His faith and determination helped him through.

So how do you handle adversity? It all comes down to free will, which I will elaborate on later in the chapter.

Sometimes when I'm hit by adversity such as depression,

disappointment, or loneliness, I will often say to myself, "You have a choice. You could choose to sit and stew through all this and be miserable, or you can choose to be happy." Once I have chosen to be happy, (and there were a few times I chose to be miserable), I find some action to foster the happiness I want.

How does this apply to entrepreneurs? Let's say you're celebrating because you're on top in your company, and a major merger helps your company grow. But that same day, a partner decides to leave, taking some of your customer base with him.

You can choose to be happy. Find ways to market to new customers, and celebrate anyway. Life happens that way. As Delatorro McNeal says, "Celebrate YOU!" He goes on to say that depending on others to celebrate, or generate happiness, is asking too much. Give it up, and make yourself happy.

Now I will divulge a personal adversity that really sent me searching for answers. In 1999, I was enduring a hard divorce. The sadness and anger I was feeling led me to question why adversity happens to people. I didn't blame my ex-wife much, but I disliked the people and situations that led to the end of my marriage. For two years I floundered around, looking for answers, crying, and showing anger. It was being terminated from a volunteer job that was the last straw. For two days I cried, then made a determination to find my answer to why there is adversity.

One morning I was getting ready for the day, when I received a spiritual insight that blew me away. The answer, (and this wasn't what I thought it would be), was one set of verbs: Choose, and Act. If you're an entrepreneur going through personal and business adversity it's up to you, you have a choice, you can make this bitter or better for you. When adversity strikes, think about your options to act. You would be surprised. It was the divorce and job termination that would later lead me to my life's work, being an author and motivational speaker. So act! Don't react. If you react to your adversity, you will get distracted- mired in a pool of negativity. But if you choose and act wisely, your business, your personal life will be on top again.

You say, "Jimmy, how can you know how I feel? My advertising business dipped in its quarterly profits, I'm mortgaged up to my eyeballs, and stuff isn't good at home." No, I certainly do not know how you feel, but I have been down the dark pit of adversity and endured the refiners fire.

Look at it this way. Adversity from a business reverse can take you out of one business model and put you in another that better suits you. I've tried three different business models and failed miserably. But the fact of the matter is everybody falls down. It's important to get back up, choose, and act.

How did I choose to handle my last business failure? My plan was to go into a business doing what I do best- a career in public motivational speaking.

It has been said, "If you never failed, you never tried enough." When I think of this, I think of Abraham Lincoln. He is one of the Presidents of the United States that touched me when I read his biographies. He lost his business, his wife was ill, plus he experienced depression. He lost eight elections- eight. Yet he persisted until he was elected President in 1860. Remember my formula for overcoming adversity. First, Choose. Choose what things are appropriate that might help you overcome your pit of adversity. Then act.

The entrepreneurial adventure is not for the fainthearted. Any step you take in business affects how you respond to adversity

Let's say you bought a pricey piece of real estate for people to rent. At first, things were good, your investment seemed sure, and the tenants liked being there. But fast forward three years later. An economic bust happens in your area, and tenants are thinking about moving elsewhere.

You try to keep the tenants you have, and market for replacements for those who do leave. Yet you can't seem to understand what went wrong. You keep holding on to the pricing you had when the market was in a boom, but this only leads you to losing more tenants.

Do this, choose to act. Say, "I may have failed this business model, but I will try again." That's all you have to do, remember, Choose and Act.

In conclusion, I hope you are open minded enough to discover my answer for adversity. Adversity has been a friend and a teacher for the 49 years I've lived on this planet. It has been used for my good. Ambiverts must discover how to be creative, how to stay positive, and then choose and act, to help overcome both their small and their deepest adversities.

In Conclusion

Congratulations! Well, look at you! You can finish the book in pride. I told you that this book would lead you to a great adventure in the characteristics of the Winning Personality. We went through what is a true ambivert. We talked about leadership and leadership vs. management. You've hit the motherload in further studies on entrepreneurship, the art and necessity of being creative. The adventure had an interesting vista in this book.

So now it's up to you! How will you apply what you have learned in this book? How will you stand in the storm clouds of adversity? Do you have the ethics, character, and fortitude it takes to make a great entrepreneur? It's not about being the best entrepreneur alone, it's about bringing the attributes you need for this creation age.

Now go out and pursue your passion!

Epilogue

This is an appendix, if you will, of the latest adversity in my life. It is a battle of wits and a battle of wills that at times I still fight today.

In April of this year, 2019, I was at an Odessa Toastmasters meeting. Unaware of what was going on in my body, I suddenly collapsed. I later learned that I had fractured my skull and had a traumatic brain injury.

Before surgery, doctors told family and friends that there were two possibilities. I would not survive surgery, or I would wake up paralyzed. No one knew what was going on inside my head for a few days after surgery. I was seeing things and hearing things that were very traumatic: thunderings and lightnings, a laser light show, people screaming. I even heard people talking nonsense. Finally I was transferred to Critical Care Unit. I had one final traumatic hallucination when my ministering brother and bishop from Church got a nurse to wake me up and calm me down. She piped in classical music to calm me down. It was still a mental battle at times, and sometimes I felt like giving up. But I told myself, "Jimmy, no matter what, you have to get up and fight!"

Things got better when I got into the skilled nursing and rehab facility in Big Spring, TX ran by my brother-in-law's mother. The physical therapists challenged me mentally and physically.

But I still battled deep loneliness and homesickness. Three things got me through all of that: the Atonement of Jesus Christ, the comfort of the Holy Ghost, and priesthood power.

The nursing home finally got me a power cord for my laptop computer, and I started writing and researching, challenging my mind. The physical therapists were intrigued by what I was writing and reading. One of them was blown away to find me reading The Book of Mormon. But I felt friends, family, and angels cheering me on through my whole ordeal.

I'm not saying I am out of the woods as far as my adversity. There are days when I still have trouble processing mentally, I think things are moving too fast. To challenge myself mentally, I returned to Toastmasters five days after returning home. Tonight I am celebrating making my first speech just fresh out of the nursing home. Writing and practicing the speech has challenged me mentally, and made things somewhat easier to process.

And this is my winning personality, and how I overcome adversity.

James Hendrick
Odessa, Texas
June 12, 2019

ABOUT THE AUTHOR

James Anthony Hendrick, Jr. is a motivational speaker, author, blogger, and podcaster. Despite being born blind and told by experts that he could not learn, James went to college and received a bachelors degree in Political Science from Texas Tech University as well as a bachelors degree in Communications from University of Texas - Permian Basin. James is active in his church, the Church of Jesus Christ of Latter-Day Saints, and his local Toastmasters group. He resides in Odessa, Texas.

www.ingramcontent.com/pod-product-compliance
Lightning Source LLC
Chambersburg PA
CBHW070130240526
45468CB00002BA/762